T0159058

THE SHEPHERDESS

A BOOK FOR PASTOR'S AND MINISTER'S WIVES

DR. JOHN THOMAS WYLIE

authorHOUSE®

AuthorHouse™
1663 Liberty Drive
Bloomington, IN 47403
www.authorhouse.com
Phone: 1 (800) 839-8640

Published by AuthorHouse 11/06/2018

ISBN: 978-1-5462-6770-6 (sc)
ISBN: 978-1-5462-6769-0 (e)

CONTENTS

A Special Dedication

This publication is dedicated to my loving wife, Angela G. Wylie, Salem Missionary Baptist Church, Lilburn, Georgia, Richard B. Haynes, Senior Pastor, Former First Lady, Mother Clara J. Copeland, wife of the Late Reverend Dr. John L. Copeland, Former Pastor of The Zion Baptist Church, Nashville, Tennessee, Former First Lady, Sister Servella Terry, wife of the Late Reverend Jimmy Terry, Pastor of the Tabernacle Missionary Baptist Church, Clarksville, Tennessee, First Lady Beverly Haynes, wife of Reverend Dr. Richard B. Haynes, Senior Pastor of Salem Missionary Baptist Church, Lilburn, Georgia and the many wives of pastors and ministers in every facet of the Christian community across the globe.

Their work is one of importance to the ministry of their husbands who God called out from the called out ones. Their contributions to their husband's effectiveness cannot be overestimated. Many times congregations expect the minister to produce effectively in a spiritual manner but overlook the efforts of their wives who are supportive of the work of their pastor or minister-husbands.

It would do us well to recognize the first ladies, or the minister's wives, pastor's wives as an effective tool God has placed in the present of the people her husband pastors or ministers. I ask myself, who can find a virtuous woman? Look at the minister's, preacher's or Pastor's Wives, who so diligently works alongside her husband as God intends, and in her own spiritual authentic character. A Minister's Wife? Yes, indeed! One of the highest privileges and rarest opportunities ever afforded God any woman.

Reverend Dr. John Thomas Wylie

INTRODUCTION

"The Shepherdess:"
A Book For Pastor's and Minister's Wives

No investigation of shepherd-pastor or minister, preacher would be complete without a part on the shepherdess. The significance of her commitment to her better half's adequacy can't be overestimated. It is my expectation that each minister, pastor or forthcoming minister, pastor will make this material required reading for his helpmate Those women who are wives of pastors, ministers, or preachers ought to likewise benefit profoundly from this reading. My significant other is the queen of our parsonage and is dealt with all things considered with all due respect that she is.

CHAPTER

ONE

Who Is The Minister's Wife?

She is a woman of God who began to look all starry eyed at and wedded a righteous man of God called "Reverend," "Minister," "Pastor" a congregation leader, a pulpiteer, a pastor, clergyman of the Gospel of Jesus Christ. She's alluded to as a first lady, yet regularly she's a young woman new out of school (college education is not a necessity for being a first lady or minister's wife, but being led by the Spirit of God is).

A couple of months, or even years prior she was considering nursing, teaching, secretarial, or some other calling. Presently she's setting out upon her new profession as a pastor's or minister's better half. She's not all beyond any doubt what this involves. Is it true that she is sufficiently arranged? No theological college has seen her female figure walking its hallways. Religious philosophy, open talking, morals, and brain sciences are subjects very unfamiliar to her.

She feel fervor and excitement, yet a genuine feeling of worry as well. Recently she was just Joann, Elaine, Betty, Esther, Ruth. Today she's

Mrs. Wylie, Mrs. Wilson, Mrs. Copeland, Mrs. Haynes, Mrs. Terry, Mrs. Sharp. Why? Since she's currently the clergyman's significant other. That makes her somebody set apart of whom many will called "First Lady", Or "Sister." That makes her someone God has set apart.

She all of a sudden ends up performing from a platform with a recolored glass window for scenery. She's relied upon to have an impact in a content she's never perused. Open correspondence in prayer is something spic and span for her. Social excitement in the house should be a simple, cheerful affair for her. Yet, in the past her mom may had accepted full accountability for this, a friend, or someone else abandoning her uninitiated.

In any case, she will learn. Since the Lord drove her down this specific way, He will similarly as unquestionably deal with the points of interest. Training currently turns into a lifestyle for her. She's mindful so as not to obliterate but rather to save her own personality, her singularity. She endeavors hard, not for mimicry but rather for her Master (Jesus Christ). Not to make a duplicate but rather by God's assistance to build up her own real-authentic character. Her life isn't a simple one, however it will dependably be a decent one. Her psychological state of mind will make it so. She appreciates a feeling of satisfaction, however she knows dissatisfaction also. Her days are exhaustingly occupied, yet they are as variable and vivid as a recently shaped rainbow.

She's the godly woman who vowed to walk as an inseparable unit with God's blessed minister. "Whither thou goest, I will go." Small assemblies or vast ones, it truly doesn't make a difference. It's wherever God coordinates that they go. Each move implies an alternate parsonage-some maybe to a great degree dazzling, some unbelivably plain. In any case, she figures out how to make it something beyond another house. It is their home.

She sees with acumen and sympathy the general population who make up her procession of life...the honest and otherworldly the flippant and callous;...the outgoing individual the self observer; ...the liberal the insatiable; - the haughty-the bothered; - the powerless-the strong;...the poor-the pleased. They are all there-seeking her for profound direction, a declaration of affection, an expression of support. In any case, she isn't the special case who gives.

She is presumably the beneficiary of more love, attention, and thoughtfulness than some other women in her assembly. God's people are so good!

She may not be a woman of irregular magnificence or have the appeal of brilliancy, however she can know the appeal and excellence of earnestness, goodness, and decontaminate. She can understand the genuine importance of beauty as the reflection from her life of blessed living gives new significance, expectation, and reason to others. She would so be able to hone the nearness, the presence of Jesus Christ in her life that her better half, her children, her parishioners may state of her, "Behold, the handmaiden of the Lord."

A Minister's Wife? Truly, without a doubt! One of the most noteworthy benefits and rarest open doors ever afforded any woman.

The Successful Shepherdess

In watching evangelists, priests, pastors and ministers it has been fascinating to take note of that diligent work, genuine devotion, and profound spiritual knowledge regularly lift the "less inclined to succeed" a long ways past or more those having each outward preferred standpoint for achieving the most for Jesus Christ. Presently the inquiry comes, "Where does the minister's wife fit into this picture?" She may contemplate internally, "I'm just the pastor's better half."

Being the minister's wife makes you extraordinary and vital piece of your better half's entire world. In spite of the fact that it's valid that a spouse will be constrained in practicing her impact in a few territories, I earnestly trust that under God she can be his most noteworthy resource from multiple points of view. We are expecting, obviously, that your devotion to Jesus Christ disposes of any unworthy intentions, endeavors at self-glorification, or conceited desire. Such would be terrible.

As we walk together through the following pages, how about we analyze a portion of the manners by which your services might be made viable and contributive to the accomplishment of our minister and shepherd-husbands. I have endeavored to maintain a strategic distance from the trite and customary for the down to earth, individual ideas which I have learned by both experience and perception. It is my petition that they may turn out to be useful to shepherdess youthful and more established who are concentrate to show themselves approved unto God.

Be Yourself

God made you "unique" with an identity, potential, and normal capacities that are exceptional to you as it were. Your significant other wedded you for your identity and what you speak to him through Jesus Christ. Truly, and for what he might be a direct result of you.

This does not imply that you should ever go to a stagnation point in the advancement of your aggregate being. Under God a nonstop change and development example ought to be acknowledged in each aspect of your life. Your psychological disposition toward life all in all is of indispensable significance. Particularly huge is the means by which you respond to your obligations as a minister's significant other.

In spite of the fact that it's conceivable to

benefit from watching the great characteristics in someone else's character, you ought to never enable yourself to get under subjugation to anybody, either inside or outside the congregation. To do as such will just impede the viability of your administration for Christ and the congregation.

I jump at the chance to picture Christian character as not based on the establishment of a solitary quality but instead on a three-dimensional base settled on up of choice, heading, and devotion. When we settle on a choice to go Christ's direction, we develop a correspondence with the Lord in which He turns out to be genuine to us as well as He is basically the genuine significance of life itself. It's just as He turns into the Master of our life that He would then be able to coordinate any of us. Since none of us can do everything great, we should essentially limit the extent of our exercises all together for the powers of our lives to achieve the most extreme in convenience. Being particular in our needs is an unquestionable requirement.

Decision - Decision, under His bearing, now ends up entire devotion pleasing to do His will. Our spirits would now be able to assert the Lord as our legacy. We can trust in Him. In no life is this more obvious than in that of a minister's better half who through her own particular identity serves Jesus Christ.

Act naturally - that self that is molding its element by her each activity, thought, and word. Who knows, you may even symbolize somebody's dream by simply acting naturally!!!

The Ministry: A Shared Service

From the pulpit to the parsonage there must be a gauge of leadership that will pay the cost of mental weariness and physical fatigue so as to grab the quickly passing chances of the day. The service of our Lord was an exemplary case of that no enduring good can be refined without the use of anxious vitality and real quality. One day amidst His wearisome calendar he thought that it was important to rest by the well.

On another event, a woman pained by her physical affliction connected and touched the hem of His piece of clothing, so awesome was her faith in His recuperating power. Jesus detected instantly that power had left Him.

Does this energize you?

...at the point when the man of your life finds the fields white unto gather and excessively couple of workers, making it impossible to help bear the load;...when his hours are too full and the days too short to satisfy the requests that are made of him;... when he feels somewhat regretful in light of the fact that the greatest long periods of the day are spent far from you and the family that he cherishes?

It is safe to say that you are ready to acknowledge the way that he, as well, might die of authority all together that he "may by all methods save a few?"

Be that as it may, he can't do everything independent from anyone else. You, the minister's or pastor's significant other must partake in this imperative administration. Paul may well have been talking about ministers' spouses (or considerably pastor's wives) for he stated, "Help these women for they have toiled next to each other with me in the gospel" (Phil. 4:3, RSV).

At the point when Jesus gave His life to make up for our sins that we may have everlasting life, He turned into the Fountain of Life for you.

However, the waters are streaming and the

Fountain is free, millions are passing on today of soul thirst. Could a portion of the fault be put on the shoulders of clergyman's spouses? Have clergyman's spouses been focused on the assignment of soul winning? Have you been touchy to the authority of the Holy Spirit in giving Him a chance to slacken our tongues? Have you neglected to hear the call of "I thirst" from the penniless circuitous us?

Examining, Praying, Sharing, seeing - they all turn into an essential piece of your life. Your clergyman spouse has a mission to achieve, but so do you. Not on account of you are a clergyman's significant other, but rather in light of the fact that you are a Christian; saved from transgression (sin), yet saved to an existence of service. What an obligation! What a ministry!

CHAPTER

TWO

Lend Your Influence Psychologically

Maybe your initial step of support will fall in the domain of your mentally impact on your significant other. This is the ground level from which he will get his fundamental heading for doing his God-given call to the service. From here he will dare to climb those precarious piles of life, to cross its wild streams, to go down into the dark valleys, or to exceed expectations to the most elevated statures.

Albeit any godly man must remain on the Biblical promises from which he draws strength for every day. There will be times when he will draw strength from you. The day by day exhibit of your affection, comprehension, sensitivity, and trust should make even your strength an image of support and motivation.

In the event that you are hopeful, it will be infectious. In the event that you prepare to stun the world, accept huge, and envision enormous, lovely dreams that lie in the domain of the conceivable, it ought to naturally extend your significant other's own particular goal for his work through Jesus Christ. It ought give him included trust in himself as well as should build his faith to trust that God can move a powerful mountain-that He "can do surpassing bounteously over all that...(he can) ask or think" (Eph. 3:20).

Without unpredictable bootlicking any man ought to be delighted by the clever valuation for his better half. Absolutely never falter to state, "I cherish you" "I Love you" or "I'm proud for you!" With the correct help, regard, fondness, and consideration, any pastor ought to be arranged mentally for wherever God leads in His plan for his life.

Encourage your Husband's Spiritual Deepening By Your Prayer Support

Praying together as a family, praying together as a couple, praying alone in the internal sanctum of your own heart - each is essential to any effective Christian. In any case, this is particularly valid for the minister and his significant other. Nobody is exempted from the traps of the foe, and the minister's wife ought to be aware of this reality.

Being a case of supplication before her better half and family will establish a permanent connection upon those in her family unit. Sending your better half from the parsonage each morning with the vow of your affection and petitions will lay the most ideal establishment for a fruitful, triumphant day for him. So Pray, Pray, Pray!

At that point it is basic you rouse move your spouses to invest much energy in supplication (prayer)! Keep your better half on his knees in a spirit of lowliness and reliance upon God. In the event that he asks he will understand that all that he achieves isn't in his own particular strength, but in God's. He could end up depleted in his own particular profound life and enable Satan to sneak in, destroying his life in the event that it were not for dependable praying.

Prayer is critical. Prayer will have the effect in our submission, in our triumphant living, in our fruitful service.

Help To Lift His Sights To Goals Higher Than His Own human Abilities

When we lift our sights so high that our objectives are just achievable through the "intensity of the Holy Spirit," at that point we need to perceive God at work in our middle. A few spouses have really moved the other way. Rather than empowering their spouses in their effort and confidence, they have constrained their service due to a "possessive state of mind."

They say, "I don't need my significant other to minister a bigger church." "I barely observe him now." What happens is this! God takes him to a medium size church. Or on the other hand he's gone from a medium size church to a littler and after that a still littler assemblage. Shepherdess, God needs your minister spouse to have the biggest range of prominence conceivable. Yours isn't to hinder but to help!

Despite the fact that you set out not be childish in constraining your better half's service, neither should you be liable of compelling your significant other into position chasing. Never being very happy with your significant other's status can be extremely collapsing to his certainty and confidence. truly, and to his ordinary manly self image!

I have heard church pioneers say, "A minister must make an interest for his administrations." You, the minister's better half, constitute an indispensable piece of that request. On the off chance that you are craving to facilitate the requests for your administrations, you will abstain from regularly being the predominant, stubborn woman who must have the last word about issues in the congregation.

One individual from a specific church board felt that his minister experienced issues in finishing any significant choice amid elder executive gatherings for fear his better half may express an alternate assessment when he arrived home.

Just a single commander can be in charge on the Good Ship of Zion, and that individual must be the minister (pastor), never the minister's significant other. You can, notwithstanding, assume a huge part by keeping the correspondence channels open for the trading of thoughts and the sharing of inventive ideas.

Without being either excessively bashful or excessively forceful, you can energize and challenge your better half to venture out in faith to achieve things that will increase the viability of his service.

CHAPTER

THREE

Stand Beside Your Husband In Times Of Crisis Involving The Members Of Your Church

Somebody has said that the individuals who carry daylight into the lives of others can't keep it from themselves. So set out to be glad! Offer bliss to others and watch your own particular identity bloom. On the off chance that acclaim is the soul that enlightens and stress is of the fragile living creature and decimates, at that point let us sing our tunes in the night and celebrate the Lord Jesus Christ.

Nonetheless, for a few, melodies won't come effortlessly. It is safe to say that you are ready, clergyman's significant other, to end up required with the necessities and in addition the delights of everyone around you? Jesus was. Jesus associated with the cheerful, felt for the sad, and gave of himself to the wiped out.

Your place of service may require a unique sort of devotion one that far surpasses the fundamental necessity and obligation of a minister's or clergyman's better half. This why it's basic that you channel your strength, physically and inwardly, into the zones of administration (service) which are unconventionally yours as a minister's/pastor's significant other.

Since your energy and intrigue may regularly exceed expectations your strength, permit the Holy Spirit (not individuals) to manage and coordinate what you do, how you do it, and the amount you do. This quickly demoralizes any adjustment to a specific model at times connected with those in your position. God made you. God has the first form in which you and only you will fit. God knows your potential. God knows your impediments. So live to please Jesus Christ, and He will deal with the humankind in individuals that may make it impossible for them to dependably, or always get it.

Minister's better half, you can enable your activities and thought processes to be administered by Jesus Christ. For example, a cherishing stroke given to a woman in trouble will some of the time say in excess of a volume of words talked by your better half. This isn't to think little of the viability of a minister or pastor. In any case, a merciful spouse has an extremely exceptional commitment to make in actualizing her significant other's service along these lines.

The main thing Jesus made careful arrangements to appear after His revival were His "scars"- scars that were the genuine signs of His redemptive service. May we have the capacity to state with Paul, "From consequently let no man inconvenience me: for I bear in my body the signs of the Lord Jesus" (Gal. 6:17).

Why the imprints? Since very regularly taking in originates from tears and anguish and agony. It might here and there originate from your own, or at times from sharing the melancholy of others. It is astonishing how an understanding heart can lift the overwhelming weight of another, similarly as sharing their satisfaction can add to their bliss. How exceptionally supported we are to be in a circumstance where we can loan our help and love in the two extremes.

Have A Trustworthy Tongue – Be Trustworthy

The pastor's better half/minister's significant other ought to dependably be reliable with her tongue. Graciousness in Words makes certainty, Benevolence in Thinking makes significance, thoughtfulness in Giving makes Love. These are the expressions of - Lao-TSE.

What we discuss uncovers an incredible arrangement about ourselves. Jesus Christ perceived this when He stated, "Out of the wealth of the heart the mouth speaketh" (Matt. 12:34). The Apostle James, who was definitely mindful of the intensity of the spoken word, particularly when talked without adoration for his fellowman, stated, "If any man insult not in word, the same is a flawless man" (Jas. 3:2).

Classification is an extremely holy trust. At the point when a parishioner shares an individual issue, he or she has a privilege to realize that it will never be uncovered to anybody under any conditions. An exceptional scholar and educator of youthful priests was extremely insistent now. He stated, "You are not at freedom to blunder here. On the off chance that a legal advisor and doctor watch this rule on their most consecrated respect, the amount more should a priest and spouse take after such a training." He proceeded by saying that it is an unpardonable break of morals in any calling where guiding is given.

On the off chance that this is valid, as I genuinely feel it may be, any disloyalty of certainty places such a person in a sketchy light as an otherworldly pioneer speaking to Jesus Christ. On the off chance that you substantiate yourself reliable as a clergyman's better half, its very conceivable that you will be told things that you can't talk about with such a certainty, absolutely never be liable of disillusioning that companion. not at the present time, not ever. Hold their confidence, their trust in you.

At that point there is the matter of free, indiscreet talk. We as a whole understand that the staple of most babble is talk, misleading statement, and distortion. The implicit temperament of the gossiper is communicated in the expressions of one who said to another, "There's something I should let you know before I discover it isn't t5rue." One man said of his minister's significant other, "She's a termite. She's end wherever she runs with her boisterous tongue." Nothing will annihilate a man's service more totally than this.

A congregation pioneer was once inquired as to whether he wouldn't take care of a bit of chatter that had been begun about him. He replied, "I don't have room schedule-wise. I'm excessively bustling serving the Lord. You've seen a huge canine running alongside little guys nipping at his foot rear areas.

Indeed, that is the manner in which I feel about occupied tongues that chomp away at individuals. You basically continue moving sufficiently quick to desert them. For whatever length of time that God's encompassing presence encompasses you, nobody can do or say anything that will truly touch you."

Have A Sense Of Humor

I trust God added a flavor of diversion to the idea of man that he may all the more completely appreciate the entire universe. In the event that it were conceivable to hear the enunciation of God's voice and to see His outward appearances as He addresses us, I'm certain we would find that He has this limit as well.

A decent comical inclination is the most ideal treatment for discharging those pressures and disappointments that regularly go to the minister and his significant other. In the event that you abhor the advantage of giggling with your better half and your family, work at it. Give your home a chance to be a fun place in which to live.

I heard a world missions official say that a standout amongst the most vital requirements for being an effective minister is to have a comical inclination. A generous chuckle, telling a joke on oneself, or seeing the amusing side of a circumstance, he stated, has spared numerous a ulcer from shaping or tears from streaming. His remark concerning a minister's significant other/better half was fundamentally the same as. "There is an opportunity to sob and an opportunity to giggle. May the good Lord help and secure the lady of the parsonage without humor enough to chuckle, for incredible will be her sobbing."

The spouse of any pastor must, obviously, have enough nobility of character to evade and kill anything that is unchristlike. It isn't the state of a lady's mouth that makes it wonderful; it's what leaves that mouth. So she ought to be consistent with herself and to her Lord in all way of discussion. Have some good times, yes! Snicker, yes! In any case, be a Christian woman in each feeling of the word.

CHAPTER
FOUR

Support And, If Necessary, Stimulate Your Husband In Setting Up A Systematic Study And Calling Schedule

Lamentably, a few men have never built up an affection for books or for considering. In the event that your significant other falls into this class, you may think that its beneficial to work with him fabricating his library. Encompass him with books. It's so vital that he read, read, read! by what other method can he satisfy the Lord in encouraging his flock?

Of need a minister's calendar will be more adaptable than that of numerous expert men. Notwithstanding, his better half ought not exploit the way that he doesn't punch a period clock and negligently keep him from his post of obligation, duty. Running errands, looking after children, housework has kept a few ministers at the parsonage (at home) long after they ought to have been in the congregation office.

Such a training could without much of a stretch deny them of profitable examination, limited time, or appearance time. This ought not be! On the off chance that you are to blame, teach yourself to discipline yourself. In the event that he is thoughtless about keeping an incite, customary calendar at the congregation, at that point he may require some direction and consolation from a scrupulous spouse.

You may feel your obligations ought exclude the arranging of your better half's timetable. Genuine. No minister should require the pushing of his significant other to persuade him in satisfying his God-given call. Notwithstanding, there a couple of men who will never make it except if somebody near them gives a slight push sporadically.

> "A True helpmate inside and out.
> That is a Minister's Wife!"

Let Love For Your Husband Protect Him Against Anybody Or Anything That Would Threaten His Reputation Or Damage His Influence For Christ

A few ladies will be particularly pulled in to (attracted to) ministers. There's regularly a purpose behind this. Where there's contention in the home or a genuine local issue between a couple, it's exceptionally conceivable that the lady included may find in the clergyman characteristics that she subtly wants in her own particular mate-delicacy, benevolence, understanding, sensitivity. A minister or pastor is generally absent to such a fascination since his solitary intrigue lies in aiding and building up the profound existences of his gathering.

Advising is known to be one of the risk territories. One minister's better half related this episode in certainty. At that point she stated, "It would be ideal if you don't hesitate to utilize this for instance of alert on the off chance that you can do as such without uncovering my name." This was her story:

A young woman had isolated from her better half and was experiencing enthusiastic and mental strain. She risked approaching regularly for my significant other's insight. Her contacts turned out to be excessively visit. It turned into an issue of worry to me. When I forewarned my significant other about it, he giggled and guiltlessly commented, "Honey, I do accept you're jealous."

My reaction was "Yes, I assume I am. be that as it may, it's not for the reason you think. I'm desirous for your notoriety, your impact, your service. I love you an excessive amount to enable anybody to exploit you."

Furthermore, she generally approaches him from a disposition of alert, never from one of doubt.

Your affection, devotion, regard, and complete trust ought to be a steadying power in the bustling routine of your better half's every day peaceful responsibilities.

Demonstrate Kindness And Courtesy To Your Husband

Give us a chance to envision each couple in the congregation designing their relationship after you and your better half. Would they mirror a solid, sound relationship of common love, comprehension, and regard? Would your individuals recognize something exceptionally unique in your craving to represent each cordiality and graciousness to your mate? They do watch you, you know.

Good conduct demonstrate good rearing. This is urgently required in our homes. Keenness is infectious, regardless of whether it be in our activities or our talked words. What more noteworthy happiness is there than to give of ourselves in adoring generosity to those inside our own family circle.

Once more, may I underline the significance of sustaining the adoration (love) connection between the man and woman who have been set apart by God to be a case in serving His Word.

Love is kept solid and enduring just when we shield it from being harmed and wounded by disregard, via inconsiderateness, by absence of correspondence. This God-given beauty of profound warmth between two people was never intended to decrease, but to develop and develop until the point when their lives turn into a wonderful two part harmony of Christlikeness.

CHAPTER

FIVE

Be Your Husband's Loving
And Constructive Critic

Most importantly, may I underscore the "loving" segment of this proposal. This will kill any probability of annoying or harping, both of which decimate the adequacy of one's endeavors to encourage anybody. The planning of making recommendations is likewise vital.

For example, you will never need to offer feedback to your better half promptly following any service when he might be worn out and perhaps debilitated.

Approach the subject when he's refreshed and in a mood to tune in. At that point, dependably approach him decidedly. Maybe complimenting his great focuses would be a decent opening.

One of the territories in which you can likely be of the most help is in the remedy of lectern characteristics which he has unknowingly created. Laymen will be reluctant to say such propensities, so you should. A few spouses be that as it may, have pointed out such diversions and got a negative response from their mate.

Truth be told, one spouse declined to trust that he talked more to the vacant seats in the gallery than to the general population on the principle floor. So one Sunday his better half chose to sit in the gallery alone.

Each time he raised his eyes to the gallery amid his message, she grinned and tenderly waved to him. Is it accurate to say that he was persuaded? To such an extent that he could scarcely entire his message!

Other than characteristics there are some of the time linguistic mistakes in talking. Maybe this is the most sensitive and troublesome territory in which one individual should rectify another. On the off chance that both of you perceive a need here, may I prescribe visiting a library or book shop where a plenitude of legitimate material can be found. Acquiring help from somebody who instructs or coaches in English is another plausibility.

Valuable feedback or redresses must remain inside the nuclear family. They are never communicated exposure to anybody whenever. This would mirror a demonstration of unfaithfulness to your wedded accomplice. "Revision through affection" is God's direction. May every one of us take after this example.

CHAPTER

SIX

The Parsonage And Entertaining

Have you at any point heard a clergyman's significant other say, "We're not tolerating a call to this congregation since they have a lacking parsonage"? I doubtlessly would like to think not! You may state to yourself, "I ponder what innovative power should be practiced in brightening this one?" Sometimes it gets the opportunity to be a significant test.

Parsonages come in all sizes and ages-from little "doll-houses" to roomy, four-room homes (Unless you are purchasing your own particular home). There may have been a period when peaceful lodging was an issue, however today numerous parsonages are far superior than the normal home of the assembly and are an enjoyment to see.

Be that as it may, if yours is short of what it ought to be, you may take a stab at doing what one smart shepherdess did. Their floors were exposed and the chips were a preliminary to their slithering infant. The minister talked about influencing fundamental plan for acquiring cash keeping in mind the end goal to take to care of their prompt need. Be that as it may, his significant other had another arrangement. She recommended that the following month to month executive gathering be held at the parsonage. "Make certain," she stated, "that you have them bow as they implore!"

Her arrangement couldn't have worked better. When one board part ascended from his knees, he stated, "I have a fragment in the knee of my slacks. These floors require some consideration! They ought to be covered." From there they took a visit through the parsonage and were stunned at the poor conditions under which their minister's family had been living.

Houses of worship truly shouldn't work without an advisory group to take care of such needs, yet now and then they do. Therefore, if the entryways of the parsonage are never opened to the general population of the gathering, they may never know about the requirement for refurbishing or a conceivable difference in houses.

The parsonage might be possessed by the congregation, however it must have the protection of a normal home-your home. Above all else, it ought to be a research center of affection and offer profound treatment for your own family.

No congregation action or outside engaging is sufficiently imperative to warrant the likelihood of making your youngsters feel that they are being disregarded or taking second place to the people of your gathering.

No little issue how substantial the duty, your own family should dependably start things out in your needs of love, consideration, and otherworldly direction.

Maybe we ought to solicit ourselves, first from all, what is our intention in engaging? Is it accurate to say that we are stretching out cordiality in adoration to the individuals who need Christian fellowship and consolation? While they're in our homes, would we say we are more worried about their solace and needs or about showing our capacity as a leader? It's imperative that we season our nourishment with adoration (love), for you see, great cooperation is significantly more essential than great sustenance.

Individuals could easily compare to materials. Keep in mind that Jesus stated, "In light of the fact that ye have done it unto one of the minimum of these my brethren, ye have done it unto me" (Matt. 25:40).

The decorations or furnishings in our homes ought to be for our benefit and utilize more than looks. On the off chance that something is spilled on your cover or your furniture scratched, acknowledge it (accept it). Nobody appreciates taking a gander at an unused home! I'm not, be that as it may, supporting wastefulness or messiness. It takes association, training, and tolerance, and in addition a huge bit of adoration and comprehension to run a home easily.

It's work, regardless of whether you have a group of two, four or eight. Is it a craftsmanship? Truly, in the event that you do it effectively.

There are two keys to all fruitful engaging in the home, regardless of whether it be for an extensive gathering or a little supper party.

To start with, legitimate arrangement. Everything conceivable ought to be escaped the way the day preceding. Silver, dishes, and materials ought to be checked. Numerous plates of mixed greens and treats can without much of a stretch be made the earlier day.

Besides, permit time for crises. In getting ready for any social occasion in your home, permit time for interferences and deferrals. This will wipe out any requirement for pushing a frenzy catch if startling crises introduce themselves amid the day.

To the extent the general population of your gathering are concerned, you will think that its more favorable and prudent to engage by bunches as opposed to by couples. A smorgasbord table is an amazing method for serving gatherings, for example, the congregation board, Sunday school classes, minister gatherings, showers, and so on.

The women of the congregation will need to encourage you. Let them. it's an astounding method for getting to be familiar, and you'll have a ton of fun doing it.

The amount you engage in the parsonage will rely upon a few variables, for example, the measure of your home, the offices with which you need to work, the age of your youngsters, the measure of cash accessible for engaging, your physical condition, and the amount you appreciate having individuals in your home. It takes time and work, yet everything does that is advantageous.

CHAPTER

SEVEN

Weddings

The time has wanted that most imperative and critical event when a youthful couple begins making arrangements for their wedding. Most ladies know precisely what they need and are very much educated with regards to the best possible techniques of a wedding.

Be that as it may, there will be some who lean intensely on the minister's or clergyman's (Ordained minister) spouse for motivation, data, and some assistance. In the event that you have been requested to help and don't have the essential data readily available (or in your mind), get a handbook regarding this matter from a book shop or wedding shop. It will diagram everything for you.

Frequently the lady of the hour will ask for that you cut the wedding cake. This is dependably a respect, and you will need to acknowledge it with satisfaction. In the event that this is your first experience and you need certainty, counsel a cateress. She will be cheerful to demonstrate to you precisely best practices to do it. The lady of the hour is satisfied if the front of the cake is left lovely to the extent that this would be possible. It's astonishing what number of pieces you can cut before irritating the part that the visitors see as they go by the table.

Maybe the most profitable and enduring commitment that you make to that little lady of the hour will be to ask with her and for her-accentuating the holiness of her wedding and the new duties that will before long be hers as a spouse. What a delight and fulfillment there is in serving the Lord in this exceptionally extraordinary limit as a Minister's Wife.

Funerals

When one of your parishioners loses a friend or family member, you and your better half will need to go as a couple to express your sensitivity and offer your services to the family. It will likewise be an open door of chance for the congregation to impart its adoration (love) and concern by soothing the deprived group of nourishment readiness.

This might be supported through the social board of trustees of the congregation, or you may incline toward working through a Sunday school class or evangelist gathering, missionary group. How much sustenance is taken to the family amid the interceding days before the burial service ought to be left to the carefulness of the group.

Nonetheless, it is standard for the congregation to give the whole dinner upon the arrival of the burial service.

You will need to conform to the desires of the family all around conceivable by counseling with them with regards to the most advantageous time and place for serving the supper. Some will favor eating in their own particular home instead of setting off to a fellowship corridor in the congregation.

A few people have been conveyed to an individual information of Jesus Christ inside their own particular hearts since God's people stretched out benevolence to them amid an emergency or time of loneliness. May every last one of us set aside opportunity to "give some cold water in His name."

Conclusion

We began with the inquiry; now we close with a similar inquiry:

"Who is the Minister's Wife?"

She's numerous things to numerous individuals. She watches over her better half's needs, offers direction to her children, keeps her home all together, but then holds time to give of herself to others. She wouldn't trade her lifestyle for any other individual's on account of the compensations of euphoria and satisfaction far surpass any short lived snapshots of debilitation and disappointment. She depends always on the power of the Holy Spirit to give her knowledge, heading, and strength for every day's walk with Him.

BIBLIOGRAPHY

Breeden, M. (2015) The Minister's Wife: Called For A Purpose. Norfolk, VA.:

CreateSpace independent Publishing Platform And IBL Media Group

Benton, A. (2017) The Minister's Wife: Privileges, Pressures And Pitfalls. USA: UK: Society For Promoting Christian Knowledge Publishers

Brister, C. W. (1964) Pastoral Care In The Church. New York, NY.: Harper And Row

Craig, F. A (1969) Christian Communicator's Handbook. Nashville, TN.: Broadman Press

Adam's, J. C. (1975) Shepherding God's Flock. Philadelphia, PA.: Presbyterian And Reformed Publishing Co.

Dicks, R. L. (1944) Pastoral Work And Personal Counseling. New York, NY.: The Macmillian Company

Floyd, J. (2009)10 Things Every Minister's Wife Needs To Know. Green Forest, AR.: New Leaf Press

Miles, C. Austin (1934) Hymns/Songs. Philadelphia, PA.: Hall-Mack Co.

Qyayle, W. A. (1910) The Pastor Preacher. Concinnati, OH.: Jennings And Graham

Oyedepo, F., Oyedepo, D., And Oyedepo, D. (2008) The Effective Minister's Wife. Nigeria, Africa: Dominion Publishing

Rogers, J. (2013) Chosen To Be A Minister's Wife. USA: Innovo Publishing

Trueblood, D. E. (1971) The Future Of The Christian. New York, NY.: Harper And Row

Wise, C. A. (1966) The Meaning Of Pastoral Care. New York, NY.: Harper And Row

The New Combined Bible Dictionary And Concordance (1984). Dallas, TX.: American Evangelistic Association

The Holy Bible (1964) Authorized King James Version. Chicago, Ill.: J. G. Ferguson

The Holy Bible (1953) The Revised Standard Version. Nashville, TN.: Thomas Nelson & Sons (Used By Permission)

The Holy Bible (1901) The American Standard Version. Nashville, TN.: Thomas Nelson (Used By Permission)

The Holy bible (1959) The Berkeley Version. Grand Rapids, MI.: Zondervan (Used By Permission)

The New Testament In Modern English (1958) J. B. Phillips, Macmillan (Used By Permission)

The New Testament In The Language Of The People (1937, 1949) Chicago, Ill.: Charles B.Williams, Bruce Humphries, Inc, Moody Bible Institute (Used By Permission)

ABOUT THE AUTHOR

The Reverend Dr. John Thomas Wylie is one who has dedicated his life to the work of God's Service, the service of others; and being a powerful witness for the Gospel of Our Lord and Savior Jesus Christ. Dr. Wylie was called into the Gospel Ministry June 1979, whereby in that same year he entered The American Baptist College of the American Baptist Theological Seminary, Nashville, Tennessee.

As a young Seminarian, he read every book available to him that would help him better his understanding of God as well as God's plan of Salvation and the Christian Faith. He made a commitment as a promising student that he would inspire others as God inspires him. He understood early in his ministry that we live in times where people question not only who God is; but whether miracles are real, whether or not man can make a change, and who the enemy is or if the enemy truly exists.

Dr. Wylie carried out his commitment to God, which has been one of excellence which led to his earning his Bachelors of Arts in Bible/ Theology/Pastoral Studies. Faithful and obedient to the call of God, he continued to matriculate in his studies earning his Masters of Ministry from Emmanuel Bible College, Nashville, Tennessee & Emmanuel Bible College, Rossville, Georgia. Still, inspired to please the Lord and do that which is well-pleasing in the Lord's sight, Dr. Wylie recently on March 2006, completed his Masters of Education degree with a concentration in Instructional Technology earned at The American Intercontinental University, Holloman Estates, Illinois. Dr. Wylie also previous to this, earned his Education Specialist Degree from Jones International University, Centennial, Colorado and his Doctorate of Theology from The Holy Trinity College and Seminary, St. Petersburg, Florida.

Dr. Wylie has served in the capacity of pastor at two congregations in Middle Tennessee and Southern Tennessee, as well as served as an

Evangelistic Preacher, Teacher, Chaplain, Christian Educator, and finally a published author, writer of many great inspirational Christian Publications such as his first publication: ***"Only One God: Who Is***

He?" – published August 2002 via formally 1st books library (which is now AuthorHouse Book Publishers located in Bloomington, Indiana & Milton Keynes, United Kingdom) which caught the attention of **The Atlanta Journal Constitution Newspaper.**

Dr. Wylie is happily married to Angel G. Wylie, a retired Dekalb Elementary School teacher who loves to work with the very young children and who always encourages her husband to move forward in the Name of Jesus Christ. They have Four children, 11 grand-children and one great-grandson of whom they are very proud. Both Dr. Wylie and Angela Wylie serve as members of the Salem Baptist Church, located in Lilburn, Georgia, where the Reverend Dr. Richard B. Haynes is pastor.

Dr. Wylie has stated of his wife, "she knows the charm and beauty of love, sincerity, goodness, and purity. She realizes the true meaning of loveliness as the reflection as her life of holy living gives new meaning, hope, and purpose to that of her husband, her children, others may say of her, "Behold the handmaiden of the Lord."

Printed in the United States
By Bookmasters